# Java

## A practical beginners guide to learn java programming, fundamentals and code

Will Norton

# Text Copyright © [Bill Norton]

## Legal & Disclaimer

The information contained in this book and its contents is not designed to replace or take the place of any form of medical or professional advice; and is not meant to replace the need for independent medical, financial, legal or other professional advice or services, as may be required. The content and information in this book has been provided for educational and entertainment purposes only.

The content and information contained in this book has been compiled from sources deemed reliable, and it is accurate to the best of the Author's knowledge, information and belief. However, the Author cannot guarantee its accuracy and validity and cannot be held liable for any errors and/or omissions. Further, changes are periodically made to this book as and when needed. Where appropriate and/or necessary, you must consult a professional (including but not limited to your doctor, attorney, financial advisor or such other professional advisor) before using any of the suggested remedies, techniques, or information in this book.

Upon using the contents and information contained in this book, you agree to hold harmless the Author from and against any damages, costs, and expenses, including any legal fees potentially resulting from the application of any of the information provided by this book. This disclaimer applies to any loss, damages or injury caused by the use and application, whether directly or indirectly, of any advice or information presented, whether for breach of contract, tort, negligence, personal injury, criminal intent, or under any other cause of action.

You agree to accept all risks of using the information presented inside this book.

You agree that by continuing to read this book, where appropriate and/or necessary, you shall consult a professional (including but not limited to your doctor, attorney, or financial advisor or such other advisor as needed) before using any of the suggested remedies, techniques, or information in this book.

# Table of Contents

# INTRODUCTION

The history of Java dates back to 1991 when programmers Patrick Haughton, Mike Sheridan, and James Gosling thought of a programming language that could best be used for the development of Digital TV. However, it was deemed to be way ahead of its own time, and thus, they redeveloped it based on the C+ and C++ platforms to make it easier and more economical to use.

With the redevelopment also came the core principles of Java, which are:

It has to be portable—or that it should work on as many platforms as possible, without any of them not working as well as the other;

It should be safe and secure to use—and definitely well encrypted;

People should feel connected to it in as little time as possible, which means that they should be working with words that are somehow familiar to them, and even though it looks complex at first, sooner or later, they have to realize that it actually works;

It should be dynamic, should work in threads, and could be modified when needed, and;

It should perform with precision.

As you can see, these core principles give you the feeling that the programmers real made Java for the people—so they can enjoy using more programs without having to buy too many devices.

In 1995, Sun Microsystems finally released Java 1.0—the first public inception of Java, which had amazing security, no-cost runtimes, and file access restrictions across all networks. Over the years, 7 more Java releases had been made, and ever since 2006, Java started to be available through GNU, or General Public License—meaning it is now a free, open-source programming language. This stemmed from the public outcry that happened once when some of its contents were made private and only available for a fee, which definitely does not resonate with its core principles.

Start reading this book now and you'll learn more about Java in no time!

# Chapter 1: What is Java?

Java is a programming language that is built by Sun Microsystems, which was later taken over by the Oracle Corporation. It is designed to run on any operating system that supports Java. This is what made the language so popular, because the developer just had to write the program once, and the program could then run on any operating system without the need for the programmer to change the code.

Most of the modern applications built around the world are made from the Java programming language. Most of the server side and business logic components of major applications are built on the Java programming language.

During the entire course of this book you will learn how to write programs such as the one above, and also learn advanced concepts that will enable you to start writing complete application programs.

Some of the design goals for Java are mentioned below:

- The language is intended to be written once and have the ability to be run on any operating system.

- The language should provide support for numerous software engineering principles.

- The language is intended to be used in developing software components suitable for deployment in distributed environments.

Portability is an important factor. This is why Java has the ability to run on Windows, Linux and the MacOS operating system.

Support for internationalization is very important.

Java is intended to be suitable for writing applications for both hosted and embedded systems.

Other design goals are discussed next:

## 1.1 Strong Type Checking

Java is a strong type language. Every variable that is defined needs to be attached to a data type.

You don't need to understand the complete program for now, but let's just have a quick look at 2 lines of the code.

1)  int i=5;

Here we are defining something known as a variable, which is used to hold a value. The value that can be stored depends on the data type. In this example we are saying that 'i' is of the type 'int' or Integer, which is a number data value.

Array Bounds Checking

At runtime, Java will check whether the array has the required number of values defined. If one tries to access a value which is outside the bounds of the array, an exception will be thrown.

You don't need to understand the complete program for now, but let's just have a quick look at the following lines of the code.

1)  int[] array1 = new int[2];

Here we are declaring an array, which is a set of integer values. The value of '2' means that we can only store two values in the array.

2) array1[0] = 1;
   array1[1] = 2;
   array1[2] = 3;

With this code we can see that we are assigning 3 values to the array. When you run this program, you will get an error because the program will see that the array has gone out of its maximum allowable bounds of two. You will get the below error at runtime.

Exception in thread "main"
java.lang.ArrayIndexOutOfBoundsException: 2

at HelloWorld.main(HelloWorld.java:8)

# Chapter 2: Why Java is important?

Next, Java has syntax and features that resemble other programming languages like C and C++. If you have any prior programming experience, you will find learning Java a breeze. Even if you are totally new to programming, you can rest assured that Java is designed to be a relatively easy language to learn. Most programmers find it easier to learn Java than say, C or C++.

Java is also designed to be platform independent. As mentioned earlier, Java code is compiled into bytecode first, which can be run on any machine that has the Java Virtual Machine.

Hence with Java, you can write the code once and run it anywhere you want.

Next, Java is an object-oriented programming (OOP) language. Object-oriented programming is an approach to programming that breaks a programming problem into objects that interact with each other.

We'll be looking at various object-oriented programming concepts in this book. Once you master Java, you will be familiar with these concepts. This will make it easier for you to master other object-oriented programming languages in future.

# Basic Tips

How has java become so successful? Java is such a widespread language for many reasons, and it owes a lot around the key principles it was designed around. One of the first principles of Java is its ease of use.

The fundamentals of the Java programming language were adapted from C ++, another extremely popular higher – level programming language.

However, though C ++ and its predecessors, C and C # are powerful languages, it tends to be rather complex in terms of syntax, and is not fully adapted for some of the purposes of Java, notably for internet technology integration.

Java thus was able to base itself on C ++, and build on this powerful language's fundamentals in order to provide a language that is also similarly powerful, but easier to use and better – suited for some specialized users.

Java is also a very reliable programming language, intentionally build in order to reduce and even eliminate the possibilities of fatal errors that arise from programmer errors. This is why Java heavily relies on object – oriented programming principles, which allows the data and the manipulation of data to be packaged together, making Java more robust and reliable, as well as much more modular, allowing for code packages to be switched out and adapted as needed.

In addition to the previous qualities of ease of use and reliability, given Java's nature of initially being designed for mobile devices, it was designed to be able to provide a higher level of security and safety for its programming, as it was initially meant for mobile devices, which by their nature are meant to exchange data over networks, making data security of the utmost priority.

Due to this, Java has become one of the most secure programming languages widely available today, making it a highly attractive option to those who wish to write programs that are less vulnerable to exploits.

Also, though Java was initially intended for mobile devices, Java has developed into a relatively platform – independent programming language, something that works to its advantage, as programs written in Java tend to work no matter what machine is running the program.

Java was written as a language that would be portable and work cross – platform, meaning that it doesn't matter what operating system the machine has, what hardware the machine is running, or what device it's running on.

This has led to its adaptability and its widespread use around the world. Due to these core principles prioritized by the Sun Microsystems team that developed Java: Ease of Use, Reliability, Safety, Cross – platform adaptability, Java became and still remains one of the most popular and most widely used programming languages today.

# Why Java?

Of course, one of the key reasons to use Java is its focus on Object – oriented programming.

Object – oriented programming, or "OOP" is a type of programming language model which allows the program's code to be organized around data, rather than functions and logic, which is known as procedural programming.

These "data clusters" are organized into things called "objects", hence the moniker of "object – oriented programming".

These objects are created by something called "classes", understood here in the traditional sense of how classes are: types of objects, allowing the programmer to "classify" them according to two major criteria: attributes and methods.

The attributes of a class are the raw data that will create the object: these are its descriptors, such as the values that it possesses, and other relevant data that will make up the object. The second criterion is the "method" of the object.

This "method" is the behavior, or the logical sequences contained within the class, describing how it interacts or can be interacted with natively.

# Chapter 3: Basics of Java

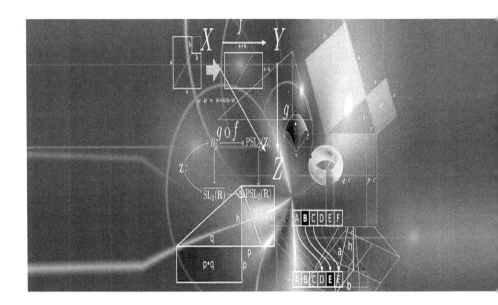

## Java tokens

Java tokens are the values that are smaller than other integers.

These numbers are going to fall between the value of -32768 and 32767. The code that I have been using is not going to work for shorts, instead I am going to need to use the short function so that I can make sure that the values are going to fall between the set limitations.

Large values are going to be stored inside of a double value along with floating point values.

A double does not have to be used if I can use a floating point.

As I am storing a floating variable. I am going to need to put a letter at the end of my value amount. This value should be f because it is a floating point number.

# Keywords

In Java, the Boolean type refers to false or true values. Java finds out if it is true or false using the reserved keywords. Therefore, an expression Boolean type will assume one of these values. An example to demonstrate include:

There are a few things to note about this program.

First, the **println(),** displays a boolean value.

Secondly, the boolean values control the flow of an if statement.

You don't need to go the long way in writing the boolean type this way: **if (b == true)**

The result shown by the operator such as < is boolean.

It is one of the reasons why we have the expression **11 > 8** showing the value **true**.

In addition, the other pair of parentheses near the **11 > 8** is important since plus comes before the >.


# Identifiers

The top layer of the diagram above is for the identifier or name. This top layer is the name you give to a class.

The name should specifically identify and also describe the type of object as seen or experienced by the user.

In simple terms, the name or identifier should identify the class.

# Operators

Java has an extensive list of operator environment.

If you are wondering what an operator is, you can look at it as a symbol which conveys a specific message to the compiler to carry out a logical or mathematical operation. I

n Java, you will interact with four classes of operators.

The four classes include:

- **Logical operator**

- **Bitwise operator**

- **Relational operator**

- **Arithmetic operator**

Like other computer languages, Java has a defined list of additional operators to take care of certain specific scenarios.

When it comes to learning JAVA programming language, or any programming language for that matter, there are five basic concepts you must understand before you get started.

These five basic concepts include:

1. **Variables**

2. **Data Structures**

3. **Control Structures**

4. **Syntax**

5. **Tools**

Each of these concepts will be thoroughly explained on a beginner's level to ensure that they are understood.

# Separators

**They are not suitable for high-level abstraction**: note that a lot of these programs make use of low-level constructs which are primarily used for low-level abstraction.

The usual approach with these programming languages is that they focus on the machine – how to make a computer do something rather than how these functions can help solve the issues of a user.

These languages deal with the minute details, which is already beyond the scope of high-level abstraction, which is the more common approach that we see today.

In low-level abstraction, data structures and algorithms are taken separately whereas these are taken as a whole in high-level abstraction.

# Literals

When it comes to literals in Java, we mean the fixed values which appear in the form in which human beings can read. We can say the number 200 is a literal.

Most of the time, literals can be constants.

Literals are important in a program. In fact, most Java programs use literals. Some of the programs we have already discussed in this book use literals.

Literals in Java can fall on various primitive data types.

The manner in which every literal is shown is determined by its type. Like it was mentioned some time back, we enclose character constants in single quotes such as '**c**' and '**%**'.

We define literals in integers without involving the fractional part.

For instance, 12 and -30 are integer literals.

A floating point literal should contain the decimal point plus the fractional part. 12.389 is a floating literal.

Java further permits for one to apply the scientific notation for the floating point literals.

Integer literals contain int value and anyone can initialize them with a variable of **short**, **byte,** and **char**.

## comments

When this occurs, we call the grey's comments.

In the running stages of the program, the grey's (comments) are moot.

This is to mean that you can use the comment feature to state or explain what the code you are creating wants to achieve.

You can achieve this by typing two slashes and then the comment.

Here is a sample.

//Place your single line comment here

You can have more than one comment line by doing either of the following:

//We are going to

//spread the comments into two

Or

/*
This comment spreads over two lines

*/

If you look at the comment above, you will notice that it starts with /* but ends with */

Additionally, if you look at the previous image (figure 8) you will notice that there are comments that begin with a single forward slash and two asterisks (/**) but end with one asterisks and one forwards slash; this is called a Javadoc comment.

# Chapter 4: What is Java Virtual Machine?

A virtual machine is software that emulates a physical machine. In traditional programming languages, code is compiled into machine language for a specific platform.

In Java, code is compiled into a virtual machine language called bytecode.

The JVM acts as an intermediary between bytecode and the underlying physical machine.

Every platform that supports Java has its own implementation of the JVM.

Java applications are portable because every JVM adheres to a standard interface.

The distribution package of the JVM and standard libraries is called the Java Runtime Environment (JRE).

The distribution package of the JRE and development tools, such as the compiler and debugger, is called the Java Development Kit (JDK).

Going back to the initial problem that we introduced earlier (i.e. making a compute radd 1 + 1), now we have a set of instructions (i.e. your algorithm) to solve the problem, the next thing you need to do is to translate that into instructions that a computer can understand.

Remember that a computer doesn't speak English or any other human language.

As it was explained earlier, you need to translate all those instructions to a series of binary signals.

But doing all that translation work will take up a lot of your time.

Remember that each character is composed of at least 8 bits.

After that you need to string them up into actual instructions to access computer memory and then do a math operations etc.—in short it's a huge mess.

No one wants to deal with that.

So, you speak a different language and the computer speaks a different one.

Well, how are you going to get both parties to meet halfway?

That is where programming languages like Java come in.

Think of a programming language as a go-between language that both computers and also human beings can understand—well so to speak, we'll clarify the details behind that in a little bit.

The goal here is to make the computer understand your instructions.

There are two phases that will happen before you can accomplish that.

The first step is to write your algorithm using a programming language. Yes, a go between language between you and the machine.

Well, computers still can't completely understand all the stuff that you will write even though it is already in Java code. And that is where step 2 comes in (2 steps remember?)—your Java code will then be processed by a program called a compiler.

As it was explained earlier when we covered the components of the Java platform, a compiler is a program or app that translates your programming code into machine readable instructions (aka instructions that your computer can understand).

There are actually a few more things that will happen in the background like a pre-compiling step as well as accessing Java libraries (mentioned earlier), then there is the actual translation into binary codes via an assembler, and more lines of code added to your original code that you wrote.

Again, all of that happens in the background.

As a Java programmer you shouldn't worry about that because the Java platform was developed to handle all of that.

It's fun to know and maybe when your programming skills have leveled up then you can go into the low level programming details yourself.

Now there is one last bit of preliminary info that you should know about before we can dive right into writing your Java programming code. And that is the Java Virtual Machine.

There is a recurring problem about the different types of hardware and software that are available in different devices today.

The hardware and software components of a smart phone will behave differently compared to that of your car or maybe your laptop.

To make things more complicated, the combination of different processor chips, different operating systems, and different arrays of electrical components will mean different ways to compile (or translate) the code you have written.

You need to make machine code specific to the platform of the device that you are programming.

## So, what is the Java Virtual Machine or JVM?

It is a program or application that is designed to run computer programs on any device or machine.

It was quite a revolutionary program when it was released in 1995 and it is still a huge innovation today.

It solved the dilemma that was described earlier.

Think of the JVM as a kind of virtual computer inside your computer. It actually has two main functions.

The first one is to run any program on any device and on any operating system or software.

This is summarized in the principle of "write once, run anywhere" – you'll hear that a lot and other programming rules of thumb as you gain more experience. T

he other function is allocating memory space—and it is very good at managing a computer's memory.

The JVM is loaded on a computer's memory (RAM). It is independent, which means it can run on any device that has support for Java—well, almost every device supports Java today.

It doesn't produce code for each type of machine, chip, and software combination out there.

That is just impossible. And even if you tried it would make Java way too large a system since you have to accommodate every type of hardware, software, and operating system there is.

## So, how does the JVM do it? I

t produces its own unique code format called bytecode.

Take note that unlike other programming languages, when your Java source code is compiled it isn't directly translated or converted into machine readable language—well, again because the goal is not to make a specific type of code that can run on only one computer platform.

The Java bytecode produced by a compiler is a set of instructions that are in machine language.

Bytecode will run on any computer that has JVM installed in it. This also means that JVM runs not just Java code and Java programs, it can also run programs written in other programming languages as well—all that is needed is for those programs to be translated (aka compiled) into bytecode.

On top of that, bytecode doesn't need to be customized so that it can be understood by different devices—as long as a device has JVM then it can run bytecode. And that is how Java can run on any device and on any computer.

Now that you have learned about the important geeky stuff, we can now move on to actual coding in Java.

# Writing Your First Java Code

Before you can write and run any Java program on your computer you need to install it on your computer first.

To install the Java Runtime Environment or JRE (i.e. the entire Java system with the JVM, the Java libraries, and all the other files), you need to go to the official Oracle corporate website by clicking here.

Instructions on how to download JRE will be provided in those web pages as well.

Some of the instructions will include temporarily disabling your firewall and what to expect during the installation process.

Now, your computer might prompt you that you don't have Java (the system that runs Java programs) installed on your computer, then you can download and install it by clicking here. Note: JRE is what you need to write Java programs, but your computer will need to install the actual Java system so that it can run Java programs.

Note that the link provided above is for the installer for Windows operating systems.

If you need to install Java for other operating systems like Mac OS X, Linux, and others, you should go here instead.

If for some reason those links don't work or you are taken to a different page, then just Google "JRE download" and then click on the link that has www.oracle.com on it.

# Required Tools

For now all you need is a text editor to write your very first Java program code.

You can use any text editor that comes with your system (e.g. Notepad if you're using Windows).

You can also use Notepad++ if you want something that has more programming support.

## IDE

However, if you want to develop applications, test your programming code, and have tools that will make programming in Java a lot easier, then you will need a program called an IDE, which stands for integrated development environment.

And IDE is an app that comes with pretty much all the facilities and tools that a programmer needs.

IDE Features

An IDE usually comes with features like autocomplete and text highlighting.

It can also be used in the building of executable files. Your Java code is usually saved as a .java file.

A compiler will then process that file and return a .class file, which is a file that you can run to test how your Java code works.

## DEBUGGING

**Debugging** is another important feature of IDEs.

Debugging refers to location and removal of programming errors on your Java source code.

No one expects you to be perfect but programming errors will prevent your code from running. IDEs have debugging tools to help you spot the errors quickly so that you can edit them ASAP.

# Best IDEs for Java Programming

There are numerous IDEs that you can use for Java programming. We can't hope to name them all so we'll just go over the top 3 IDEs.

## 1. NetBeans

NetBeans was first released back in 1997 and it can run on different operating systems like Windows, Solaris, Mac OS, and Linux. NetBeans is actually the official IDE for Java 8.

Just like Java, NetBeans is open source – that means it is free to download and use.

It features semantic and syntactic highlighting. It also allows you to refactor your source code (i.e. rewriting code making it more efficient without actually causing any programming problems).

Refactoring is done either to improve the performance of a program or to update it to the latest standards. In other words you are giving an old program an upgrade or update.

## 2. IntelliJ IDEA

IntelliJ IDEA was first released back in January of 2001. It runs on Windows, Mac OS, and Linux. This IDE comes in 2 different editions.

The first one is the proprietary aka the commercial version (i.e. the one you have to pay for) and the other one is the Apache 2 Licensed edition.

This is the IDE for really serious programmers—we suggest that you use this integrated development environment after you have gained a lot of experience programming in Java. You can call this the deep dive IDE.

Two of the unique and powerful features of IntelliJ IDEA include flow analysis and cross language refactoring. It also provides support for other JVM based languages—yes there are other programming languages that also use JVM.

## 3. Eclipse

Eclipse is another advanced integrated development environment.

In fact, this one is solely dedicated and specialized for the development of Java programs.

Well, it also supports other programming languages as well, which makes it a very powerful tool.

In case you have reached the point of being able to combine different programs written in different programming languages then you might want to consider getting this IDE.

If you are a beginner then that will be some time in the future. Now, there are two versions of Eclipse.

There is a cloud version of this IDE which is called Eclipse Che and there is the good old desktop version, which you can download on your computer.

Both of these versions come with an entire suite of tools, apps, and plugins that make programming work a whole lot easier. It even comes with its own custom compiler.

This IDE is loaded with a lot of useful features.

For instance, if you want to focus on developing plugins for programs that have already been written, Eclipse has a Plugin Development Environment.

It has all the tools you need to create and improve plugins.

There are a lot of other IDEs of course. You can find them by just Googling "best Java IDEs".

There are free IDEs and there are commercial ones as well. You can try the three mentioned here or you can investigate other IDEs out there.

The choice is yours.


Here's a short list of IDEs that you can find out there:
- **JDeveloper**
- **Greenfoot**
- **DrJava**
- **Codenavy**
- **Xcode**
- **MyEclipse**
- **BlueJ**

# Chapter 5: Basic structure of a Java Program

## Package

On the first line, we have the statement

package helloworld;

This statement tells the compiler that the Java file we wrote belongs to the helloworld package.

A package is simply a grouping of related classes and interfaces.

When we write package helloworld; at the top of our file, we are asking the compiler to include this file in the helloworld package.

The compiler will then create a folder named "helloworld" and save the file into that folder.

Files that belong to the same package are stored in the same folder.

If you navigate to your "NetBeansProjects" folder now, you'll find a folder named "HelloWorld".

The "NetBeansProject" folder is normally located in your "Documents" folder. If you can't find this folder, try searching for it using your computer's search function.

Within the "HelloWorld" folder, you'll find a "src" folder that contains the "helloworld" folder.

In addition to packages created by us, Java also comes with a large number of pre-created packages that contain code that we can use in our programs.

For instance, code for input and output is bundled in the java.io package while code for implementing the components of a graphical user interface (like buttons, menus, etc) is bundled in the java.awt package. To use these pre-written packages, we need to import them into our programs.

We'll learn how to do that at a later time.

Within the HelloWorld class, we have the main() method which starts on line 5 and ends on line 8.

The main() Method

The main() method is the entry point of all Java applications. Whenever a Java application is started, the main() method is the first method to be called.

Notice the words String[] args inside the parenthesis of our main() method? This means the main() method can take in an array of strings as input.

In our example, the main() method contains two lines of code. The first line

//Print the words Hello World on the screen is known as a comment and is ignored by the compiler.

# Chapter 6: Code structure of Java

In the figure, you should notice the package name comes first.

Additionally, you should note that a semicolon is what ends the line.

The semicolon is important and if you omit it, the program will not compile.

**package firstproject;**

Next is the class name

**public class FirstProject {**

**}**

You can use the left curly bracket at the start of a code, and use the right curly bracket to end the code {this is an example of a curly code segment} you should however note that anything that goes inside the left and right curly is part of the said code segment.

Additionally, anything inside both the left and right curly for the class is in fact, a code segment. Here is what I mean:

$$\text{public static void } \textit{main} \Big( \textbf{ String[ ] args } \Big) \ \Big\{$$

*}*

More important than anything else is the word "main". Why?

Because each time any Java program boots up, it first looks for the method bearing the name 'main'. Simply put, a method is a piece of code.

The program then executes codes within the curly as part of the main.

There are possibilities that you will get an error message within the Java program if your code does not have a main method.

However, since this is the main entry point for your program, there is little chance you will omit it.

The public part of the code (the blue part) simply means that the method is viewable outside that class.

On the other hand, static means that the creation of a new object is not necessary while void means that, there is not returnable value and the command gets on with it.

# How to download and install Java on Linux, Windows and Mac.

Check out the figure below.

Figure 10

In the NetBeans tool bar, you will notice a "green play" arrow; you can use this to run a program.

Figure 11

You can also run a program by navigating to your projects window.

This is especially effective in ensuring that the correct source code is running.

To do this, you need to click on your java source file contained in the project window and then right click for options.

Execute the run command. See figure below.

Figure 12

If you use any of the program execution methods above on our code so far, you should get something similar to figure13 below on the output window

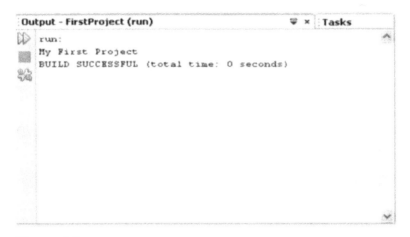

Figure 13

In figure 13 above, you can see that the first line is the run command.

The second is our code "My First Project."

If there is something you are not sure of and would like to run the code again, you can simply press the "two almost fast-forward green arrows" visible on figure 13 above.

# Chapter 7: Data Types and Variables

Of course, one of the key reasons to use Java is its focus on Object – oriented programming. Object – oriented programming, or "OOP" is a type of programming language model which allows the program's code to be organized around data, rather than functions and logic, which is known as procedural programming.

These "data clusters" are organized into things called "objects", hence the moniker of "object – oriented programming".

These objects are created by something called "classes", understood here in the traditional sense of how classes are types of objects, allowing the programmer to "classify" them according to two major criteria: attributes and methods.

The attributes of a class are the raw data that will create the object: these are its descriptors, such as the values that it possesses, and other relevant data that will make up the object.

The second criterion is the "method" of the object.

This "method" is the behavior, or the logical sequences contained within the class, describing how it interacts or can be interacted with natively.

In order to make this clearer, say that there is a class "Human". This "class" will have attributes such as height, weight, gender, race. The "human" class can also have methods such as "run", "walk", "talk". These theoretical components make up the "human" class, a blueprint for an object.

Now that the class has been defined, the programmer, if they so wish, can create an object using the "human" class as a blueprint.

They can invoke the class "Human" and "populate" its attributes, giving it a specific height, weight, gender, and race. In addition, the object already has built – in functions such as "run", "walk", and "talk", so upon the creation of an object, let's say named "Mike" from the "Human" class, it already contains the functions to run, walk, and talk, without need for the programmer to code those specific functions again, as they are already "inherent" in the created object.

In a nutshell, that is what Object - oriented programming is meant to be: a way of programming that allows the programmer to draw on pre – defined classes so that it will be easier to describe them and use their internal, or built – in functions in order to operate them.

Assuming that the reader is not a total newbie to programming, and has been introduced to the world of programming using C or another procedural – heavy language, the next logical question would be: why even use object – oriented programming?

Well, one of its main advantages is that in the long run, it saves time.

Procedural programming is usually much quicker and more straightforward in simpler algorithms and programs; rather than having to construct and define a class, and create an object based on that class, all the programmer really has to do is to simply declare the necessary variables and write the functions, and create the algorithm in order to solve the problem that they need the code to address.

However, when it comes to more complex programs, needing more complex solutions, this is where object – oriented programming begins to shine, and this is where it starts to show its strength.

In a lot of programs, there will be times that there will be a number of "objects" or data clusters that have to be grouped together, and that the programmer will be treating in a certain way.

This is what "classes" are meant to address.

Instead of declaring a new set of variables per data cluster, they can simply draw on a pre – made "class" and create a new "object".

Let's see how this would work in practice.

If a programmer were to code a chess game in procedural fashion, then they would have to manually describe each and every piece, all sixteen pawns, four bishops and four knights, four rooks, two queens, and two kings. In addition, they will have to write the functions that allow each piece to move in its own separate way.

However, if the programmer makes use of object - oriented programming, instead of having to code sixteen pawns, four bishops, four knights, four rooks, two queens, two kings, they simply have to code six classes: one class to describe each piece on the board.

The programmer can now simply include the movement functions within each class, and have the attributes describe their position: whether they're white king's pawn, or black queen's pawn, these are all things that can be inserted through the "attributes" portion of the "pawn" class. Instead of thirty – two clusters of code, the programmer only has to do six.

Now it's much easier, much shorter, and also much more elegant.

# Java tokens

Java tokens are the values that are smaller than other integers.

These numbers are going to fall between the value of -32768 and 32767.

The code that I have been using is not going to work for shorts, instead I am going to need to use the short function so that I can make sure that the values are going to fall between the set limitations.

Large values are going to be stored inside of a double value along with floating point values.

A double does not have to be used if I can use a floating point. As I am storing a floating variable.

I am going to need to put a letter at the end of my value amount.

This value should be f because it is a floating point number.

# Keywords

In Java, the Boolean type refers to false or true values. J

ava finds out if it is true or false using the reserved keywords. Therefore, an expression Boolean type will assume one of these values.

An example to demonstrate include:

There are a few things to note about this program.

First, the **println()**, displays a boolean value. Secondly, the boolean values control the flow of an if statement.

You don't need to go the long way in writing the boolean type this way: **if (b == true)**

The result shown by the operator such as < is boolean. It is one of the reasons why we have the expression **11 > 8** showing the value **true**.

In addition, the other pair of parentheses near the **11 > 8** is important since plus comes before the >.

# Identifiers

The top layer of the diagram above is for the identifier or name.

This top layer is the name you give to a class. The name should specifically identify and also describe the type of object as seen or experienced by the user.

In simple terms, the name or identifier should identify the class.

# Operators

Java has an extensive list of operator environment.

If you are wondering what an operator is, you can look at it as a symbol which conveys a specific message to the compiler to carry out a logical or mathematical operation. In Java, you will interact with four classes of operators.

The four classes include:

- Logical operator

- Bitwise operator

- Relational operator

- Arithmetic operator

Like other computer languages, Java has a defined list of additional operators to take care of certain specific scenarios.

When it comes to learning JAVA programming language, or any programming language for that matter, there are five basic concepts you must understand before you get started.

These five basic concepts include:

1. Variables

2. Data Structures

3. Control Structures

4. Syntax

5. Tools

Each of these concepts will be thoroughly explained on a beginner's level to ensure that they are understood.

# Separators

**They are not suitable for high-level abstraction**: note that a lot of these programs make use of low-level constructs which are primarily used for low-level abstraction.

The usual approach with these programming languages is that they focus on the machine – how to make a computer do something rather than how these functions can help solve the issues of a user.

These languages deal with the minute details, which is already beyond the scope of high-level abstraction, which is the more common approach that we see today.

In low-level abstraction, data structures and algorithms are taken separately whereas these are taken as a whole in high-level abstraction.

# Literals

When it comes to literals in Java, we mean the fixed values which appear in the form in which human beings can read. We can say the number 200 is a literal. Most of the time, literals can be constants.

Literals are important in a program. In fact, most Java programs use literals. Some of the programs we have already discussed in this book use literals.

Literals in Java can fall on various primitive data types.

The manner in which every literal is shown is determined by its type. Like it was mentioned some time back, we enclose character constants in single quotes such as '**c**' and '**%**'.

We define literals in integers without involving the fractional part. For instance, 12 and -30 are integer literals. A floating point literal should contain the decimal point plus the fractional part. 12.389 is a floating literal.

Java further permits for one to apply the scientific notation for the floating point literals.

Integer literals contain int value and anyone can initialize them with a variable of **short**, **byte,** and **char**.

## comments

When this occurs, we call the grey's comments. In the running stages of the program, the grey's (comments) are moot.

This is to mean that you can use the comment feature to state or explain what the code you are creating wants to achieve.

You can achieve this by typing two slashes and then the comment. Here is a sample.

//Place your single line comment here

You can have more than one comment line by doing either of the following:

//We are going to

//spread the comments into two

Or

/*
This comment spreads over two lines

*/

If you look at the comment above, you will notice that it starts with /* but ends with */

Additionally, if you look at the previous image (figure 8) you will notice that there are comments that begin with a single forward slash and two asterisks (/**) but end with one asterisks and one forwards slash; this is called a Javadoc comment.

# what are variables

A variable, on the other hand, is an "object" that contains a specific data type and its assigned or received value.

It is called a variable because the value contained can change according to how it is used in the code, how the coder can declare its value, or even how the user of the program chooses to interact with it.

A variable, in short, is a storage unit for a data type. Having access to variables allow programmers to conveniently label and call stored values at hand.

# Types of variables in Java

Java requires the programmer to use declaration statements, lines of code used to declare variables and define them by specifying the particular data type and name.

Java has a specific way of treating variables, by defining variables as containers that contains a certain type and value of information, unlike some languages such as python, which only requires a declaration of a variable, and the variable can dynamically change its type;

Java variables are **static**, which retain their type once declared.

Int number = 20;

Boolean completed = true;

String hello = "Hello World!";

The syntax in declaring is seen in the previous examples, with the type of the variable coming first, then the name of the variable, then the value.

Note as well that the declaration statement can be composed of multiple declarations in one line, as in the following example:

Int number = 20, Boolean completed = true, string hello = "Hello World!";

Java variables can be declared without any value at the start; in cases such as these, Java chooses to declare these variables with a particular default value, for example:

Byte a;

Short num;

Boolean answer;

Will result in the values 0, 0, and false, respectively.

A more complete list of default values is as follows: the byte, short, int, and long data types will all result in a default value of 0, while the float and double data types will have a default 0.0 value, the char data type will result in 'u\0000' value, a string or any other object will have a null default value, and all Booleans will begin with a false default value.

In Java, variables are static when declared, meaning that the programmer must define the data type that the variable will be containing.

To illustrate, if we wish to use a variable **num** to store a number, we would first have to declare the variable: "int **num**", before we can assign a value, such as "**num = 10**".

The process above is usually known as and referred to as an "assignment statement", where a value is **assigned** to the variable as declared by the programmer.

However, one prominent thing about how Java, and in fact how most programming languages, works is that in the assignment statement, such as in our example of num = 10, the actual value stored is the one on the right side of the equals sign, the value of 10, and num is just the "marker" to call that stored value.

This is why there are many Java programmers that tend to prefer the jargon of "getting" a value rather than "assigning", though for the most part, they may be employed interchangeably, and outside of some rare scenario, function mostly the same way.

Note, however, that once values have been assigned to variables, functions need to be carried out in order for the data inside that variable to change its data type.

# Naming a variable

Creating variables is an easy task, especially given how Java programmers tend to create and name them after the data type or the purpose of what the variable will store.

However, there are a few rules when it comes to naming these variables, else Java will not recognize it and an error message will result. The main restrictions around variable names are that it should not begin with a special character such as an underscore or a number.

However, variable names can consist of characters such as letters and numbers, and even an underscore, provided that the underscore is not placed at the start.

No other characters may be used, such as the # or even $, as these special characters have different uses in Java, and thus will not be recognized in a variable name.

While those are the major rules, here are some tips when it comes to naming variables.

The variable name should be descriptive, as in longer codes it may be difficult to recall just what "x" is for.

Having a variable name such as "count" or "output" is much easier to recall as compared to having a generic "x" or "y" and will help in avoiding confusion.

In addition to being descriptive, variables will also be easier to use if their names are kept fairly short.

While having a variable name such as banking_information_account_records is very descriptive, typing it repeatedly as needed in the program will get exhausting, and having longer variable names increase the chances of typographical errors, which will lead to bugs in the code, resulting in a run - time error or the code not working as intended, or working, but introducing bugs along the way.

Note as well that it has always been a practice for Java variables to be written in all lower – case letters, and while there is no restriction on capitalization, keeping things in lowercase simplifies things, as a missed capitalization may result in the variable not being recognized, as Java reads an upper – case letter as an entirely different character versus a lower – case letter.

# Java primitive types

## Method Naming Conventions

We shall revisit the naming conventions in Java since you will be using member methods.

Methods in Java programming perform operations, they also receive any argument provided by a caller, and it can also return a result of an operation to a caller.

Here's the syntax for declaring a method:

[Access Control Modifier] Return Type methodName ([set of parameters]) {

  // body of the method

  ......

}

Here are a few rules to remember when you make the names for the methods that you will write.

Method names are always verbs or more specifically verb phrases (which means you can use multiple words to name them).

The first word of the method name should all be in lower case letters while the rest of the words should follow a camel case format. Here is an example:

writeMethodNamesThisWay( )

Now, you should remember that verbs are used for method names, and they indicate an action while nouns are used for variable names, and they denote a certain attribute.

Following the syntax for declaring a method and following the name conventions for this Java construct, here's a sample code that can be used to compute the area of a circle.

```
public double computeCircleArea() {
return radius * radius * Math.PI;
}
```

Using Constructors in Your Code

We'll just go over some additional details as they relate to object oriented programming.

As stated earlier, a constructor will look like a method, and you can certainly think of it and treat it like a special kind of method in Java programming.

However, a constructor will still be different from a method in several ways. The name of a constructor will be the same as the class name.

Use the keyword or operator "new" to create a new instance of the constructor and also to initialize it. Here's an example using the class "Employee" and a variety of ways to initialize it in your code:

```
Employee payrate1 = new Employee( );
Employee payrate2 = new Employee(2.0);
Employee payrate3 = new Employee(3.0, "regular");
```

A constructor will also implicitly return void – that simply means it doesn't have a return type. You can't put a return statement inside the body of a constructor since it will be flagged by compilers as an error.

The only way you can invoke a constructor is via the use of the "new" statement. We have already given you several ways how you can invoke constructors in the samples above.

One final difference is that constructors can't be inherited. Let's go back to the examples provided above – the first line includes "Employee( );" – that is called a default constructor. As you can see, it has no parameters whatsoever.

The job of a default constructor is to simply initialize the member variables to a specific default value. In the example above, the member variable payrate1 was initialized to its default pay rate and employee status.

Can constructors be overloaded too? Yes, they can. Constructors behave like methods too so that means you can overload a constructor just the same way you overload a method.

Here are a few examples on how you can overload a constructor.

We use the Employee class and overload it using different parameters.

Employee( )

Employee(int r)

Employee(int r, String b)

# How to initialize a variable

Now that we know how to declare variables, and we know the various types of variables that are available to us, the next thing to do is to learn how to make use of these variables, in something called "expressions".

Expressions are the most used building blocks of a Java program, generally meant to produce a new value as a result, though in some cases expressions are used to assign a new value to a variable.

Generally, expressions are made up of things such as values, variables, operators, and method calls.

There are also some expressions that produce no result, but rather affect another variable.

One example would be an expression that changes the value of a variable based on an operation: there is no new value output, and there is no true "assignment" of a new value, but rather there is what is called a **side effect** that results in a changed variable value.

In our previous sample program above, such as the "Hello World" printing program, we introduced raw values into the print function, also known as "hard coding" the output.

However, at this point, we should try to incorporate what we have learned about variables.

Variables operate much the same way as raw values, as they simply reference a previously stored value by the computer, and as such, the programmer can just use the variable name instead of the value.

In order to demonstrate this, let us remember the previous "Hello World" program:

print ("Hello World") ;

input ("\n\nPlease press the return key to close this window.") ;

Now, instead of hard – coding the "Hello World" string, we can simply declare it into a variable and have the program output that variable.

This should end up looking as:

String = "Hello World" ;

print(string) ;

input ("\n\nPlease press the return key to close this window.") ;

This should come out with the same result as the previous program, looking something similar to:

Hello World

Please press the return key to close this window.


# **Variables modified by code**


However, the reader may be wondering why we even use a variable in this case, as it makes our code even longer.

 In very short codes, such as the classic "Hello World", using variables does make it longer, but to demonstrate how they can be used to shorten a code, let's use another code to show the usefulness of variables.

For this code, we will attempt to print out a few times table values. In this code we will be using a few iterations and loops, which will be explained further on.

Int num = 9;

byte count = 0 ;

while (counter <10) {

print(num " * ") ;

print(counter "= ") ;

```
print(num * counter "\n") ;

counter = counter + 1} ;
```

This basic snippet of code will output the multiplication table of whatever is in the num variable up until times nine. In this program we are to be incorporating a so – called while condition and an iteration function.

However, if we break down the components of the code as provided, the "while" condition tells Java to continue iterating the code beneath it until the condition is not true. Since count was initialized at a value of 0, and every time the code runs, the count variable will increase by one, the loop will run for ten times.

The code nested within the "while" condition tells the Java program to print an equation of the number multiplied by the "counter" variable, meaning that it will print ten lines, from times zero to times nine.

 The code should end up looking like the following output:

9 * 0 = 0

9 * 1 = 9

9 * 2 = 18

9 * 3 = 27

9 * 4 = 36

9 * 5 = 45

9 * 6 = 54

9 * 7 = 63

9 * 8 = 72

9 * 9 = 81


Now try and imagine how a more seasoned programmer would think of how to write an algorithm to create a similar table without having a variable that can be changed as the code runs.

They would have to "hard – code" all the values and type all the numbers just to get a simple multiplication table. However, due to the power of variables, the coder can simply assign a basic starting value and their code should do the rest.

# Variables modified by user input

Variables can have a value declared by the programmer in the code, but the programmer can also have their variables as defined by the user.

Remember that user input can be read by the Python code by the use of the input () function.

They can do this while declaring the variable, or they may wish to have their user input a new value to an already – declared variable.

Let's see how this works using the previous multiplication table code:

Int num = NextInt(input("Please enter a number from 0 – 9 to initialize the multiplication table.")) ;

Int counter = 0 ;

while (counter<10){

print(num " * ") ;

print(counter "= ") ;

print(num * counter "\n") ;

counter = counter + 1 ; }

This code prints an initial line and waits for the user to input a number before the code will run.

Note that the user can technically enter a character that is not a number, and this will result in an error.

Furthermore, the input function in this case is limited to receiving a single character, so only a number from 0 – 9 can be used, as longer digits will not be read.

The variable declaration is a nested function, ensuring that the user input will be converted into an integer, rather than having a character, allowing the code to use mathematical operations.

# Arithmetic operators

## Arithmetic operators in Java include:

- + represents addition
- - represents subtraction
- * represents multiplication
- / represents division
- % represents modulus
- ++ represents increment
- -- represents decrement

Operators such as +, -, *, and / all perform the same function just like the rest of other languages.

> We have seen that JavaScript has the ability to work with numbers. Hence it also has the ability to work with the operators that can be used with the number data type. Let's look at each of the operators in more detail.

## Arithmetic Operators

These are operators that are used to work with numbers. The most common operators are shown below, followed by an example of how it can be applied.

With this program, the output is as follows:

JavaScript Program

The first value is 5

The second value is 10

Addition operator = 15

Subtraction operator = 5

Multiply operator = 50

Division operator = 2

Increment operator = 6

Decrement operator = 5

Modulus operator = 5

# Assignment operators

These are operators that are used to determine the value of conditions based on the value of the operands.

The relational operators possible in JavaScript are given below.

If a condition evaluates to true, then a value of 1 is returned, otherwise a value of 0 is returned.

With this program, the output is as follows:

JavaScript Program

The first value is 5

The second value is 10

Are the numbers equal = false

Are the numbers not equal = true

Is x less than y = true

Is x greater than y = false

Is x greater than or equal y = false

Is x less than or equal y = true

# Logical Operators

These are operators that are used to determine the value of conditions based on the value of the operands, where the operands are Boolean values.

The logical operators possible in JavaScript are given below.

With this program, the output is as follows:

JavaScript Program

The first value is true

The second value is true

The third value is false

x AND y = true

y AND z = false

z AND x = false

z AND z = false


The table below shows the logical operators based on the value of the operands for the OR operator.


With this program, the output is as follows:

JavaScript Program

The first value is true

The second value is true

The third value is false

x OR y = true

y OR z = true

z OR x = true

z OR z = false

The following table shows the logical operators based on the value of the operands for the NOT operator.

## Assignment Operators

These are operators that are used to make assignment operations easier. The assignment operators possible in JavaScript are given below.

Now let's look at how we can implement these operators in further detail.

With this program, the output is as follows:

JavaScript Program

The first value is 5

The second value is 6

The value of i+j is 11

The value of i+=j is 11

The value of i-=j is 5

The value of i*=j is 30

The value of i/=j is 5

The value of i%=j is 5

# Bitwise Operators

These are operators that are used to make bit operations on operands.

With this program, the output is as follows:

JavaScript Program

The first value is 5

The second value is 6

The value of x AND y is 4

The value of x OR y is 7

The value of NOT x is -6

The value of x XOR y is 3

The value Zero fill left shift is 10

The value Signed right shift is 2

The value Zero fill right shift is 2

# Chapter 8: Java Data Structure and Algorithms

In order to make this clearer, say that there is a class "Human". This "class" will have attributes such as height, weight, gender, race. The "human" class can also have methods such as "run", "walk", "talk".

These theoretical components make up the "human" class, a blueprint for an object. Now that the class has been defined, the programmer, if they so wish, can create an object using the "human" class as a blueprint.

They can invoke the class "Human" and "populate" its attributes, giving it a specific height, weight, gender, and race.

In addition, the object already has built – in functions such as "run", "walk", and "talk", so upon the creation of an object, let's say named "Mike" from the "Human" class, it already contains the functions to run, walk, and talk, without need for the programmer to code those specific functions again, as they are already "inherent" in the created object.

In a nutshell, that is what Object - oriented programming is meant to be: a way of programming that allows the programmer to draw on pre – defined classes so that it will be easier to describe them and use their internal, or built – in functions in order to operate them.

Assuming that the reader is not a total newbie to programming, and has been introduced to the world of programming using C or another procedural – heavy language, the next logical question would be: why even use object – oriented programming?

Well, one of its main advantages is that in the long run, it saves time.

Procedural programming is usually much quicker and more straightforward in simpler algorithms and programs; rather than having to construct and define a class, and create an object based on that class, all the programmer really has to do is to simply declare the necessary variables and write the functions, and create the algorithm in order to solve the problem that they need the code to address.

However, when it comes to more complex programs, needing more complex solutions, this is where object – oriented programming begins to shine, and this is where it starts to show its strength.

In a lot of programs, there will be times that there will be a number of "objects" or data clusters that have to be grouped together, and that the programmer will be treating in a certain way.

This is what "classes" are meant to address. Instead of declaring a new set of variables per data cluster, they can simply draw on a pre – made "class" and create a new "object". Let's see how this would work in practice.

If a programmer were to code a chess game in procedural fashion, then they would have to manually describe each and every piece, all sixteen pawns, four bishops and four knights, four rooks, two queens, and two kings.

In addition, they will have to write the functions that allow each piece to move in its own separate way.

However, if the programmer makes use of object - oriented programming, instead of having to code sixteen pawns, four bishops, four knights, four rooks, two queens, two kings, they simply have to code six classes: one class to describe each piece on the board.

The programmer can now simply include the movement functions within each class, and have the attributes describe their position: whether they're white king's pawn, or black queen's pawn, these are all things that can be inserted through the "attributes" portion of the "pawn" class. Instead of thirty – two clusters of code, the programmer only has to do six.

Now it's much easier, much shorter, and also much more elegant.

# Chapter 9: Arrays in Java

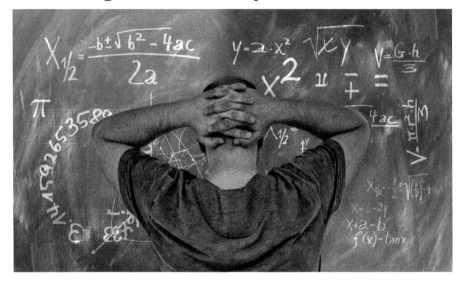

Arrays are sequences of elements; each element must be associated with one or more index positions.

Elements are groups of memory locations, each one storing one item of data.

Indexes are integers that are non-negative; in the case of the array, they are used for identifying the element associated with the index.

You can consider the relationship between the two to be similar to how a postbox number identifies a specific house on a specific street.

Usually, one element will have one index but there may sometimes be more.

The number of those indexes per element is the dimension of the array.

We are going to start by looking at one-dimensional arrays; later, we will move on to the multi-dimensional arrays.

Java has full support for arrays. Each of the elements in an array will occupy the same byte amount and the exact amount will depend on the data type of the element.

It is also worth noting at this stage that every element in one array will be of the same data type.

It is also important to note that you cannot resize a Java array; they are of a fixed size and may not be changed once they have been created.

Rather than doing this, if you needed an array to be a different size, you would need to create a new one of the correct size and then copy all the elements you need from the first array to the new one.

One-Dimensional Arrays

One-dimensional arrays are the simplest of all arrays.

In this kind of array, one element is associated with one index and the array is used for storing data items in lists.

We can use three separate techniques for creating a one-dimensional array:

- With just an initializer
- With just the new keyword
- With both an initializer and the new keyword

Using Just an Initializer

The syntax required to use an initializer to create a one-dimensional array is:

'{' [expr (',' expr)*] '}'

What this syntax says is that a one-dimensional array is a list of expressions that is optional and with each expression separated by a comma, all between a set of curly braces.

All of the expressions have got to evaluate to types that are compatible.

For example, if you had a one-dimensional array of doubles with two elements, both of those elements may be of the double type or just one may be of the double type while the other may be an integer or a floating point number.

Have a look at this example:

{ 'J', 'a', 'v', 'a' }

Using the New Keyword

The new keyword is used to allocate the array memory and return the array references. The syntax is:

'new' type '[' int_expr ']'

What the syntax tells us is that the one-dimensional array is a series of positive elements, all of int (integer) type.

All the elements in the array will be zeroed and will be interpreted as one of the following:

- 0
- 0L
- 0.0F
- 0.0
- false
- null
- '\u0000'

For example:

new char[4]

Using an Initializer and the New Keyword

The syntax required to create the array using both the initializer and the new keyword is this, a combination of the two separate syntax approaches mentioned above:

'new' type '[' ']' '{' [expr (',' expr)*] '}'

Because we can work out how many elements are in the one-dimensional array by looking at the list of comma-separated expressions, we do not need and, indeed, must nor use, an int_expr within the set of square brackets.

For example:

new char[] { 'J', 'a', 'v', 'a' }

It is worth noting that there is no difference between the syntax for using just the initializer and the syntax for using the initializer and the new keyword.

The first one, with just the initializer, is something called syntactic sugar – this just means the syntax is much easier to use.

Array Variables

On its own, a new one-dimensional array is quite useless. For it to be worth anything, we must first assign its reference to an array variable that has a compatible type and we can do this in two ways – directly or by using a method call.

The following example shows how the variable is declared:

type var_name '[' ']'

type '[' ']' var_name

Both types of syntax are declaring the variable that will store the reference to the one-dimensional array. You can use whichever type you prefer but the preferred method is the first one, with the set of square brackets after the variable type.

In these examples, there are three array variables – name1, name2, and name3. The set of square brackets is telling Java that each of those variables will store the reference to a one-dimensional array.

The keyword, char, is an indication that the elements must store values of the char type but, provided Java can do a conversion to a char, you may specify values that are non-char. For example, the following is perfectly ok because 10, a positive int, is small enough that it fits in the range for char (0 to 65535) and can easily be converted to a char:

char[] chars = { 'A', 10 };

However, the next example would not be ok because it doesn't fit in the range:

char[] chars = { 'A', 80000 };

All array variables have a length property associated with them. This property will return the one-dimensional array length, indicated as a positive int.

For example, name1.lenght would return a value of 4.

With the array variable specified, it is possible to access any one of the elements in the array and we do this by stating the expression that will agree with this syntax:

array_var '[' index ']'

In this expression, we have a positive int of index; it ranges from 0 to one lower than the length property value. Don't forget, Java indexes start at zero.

Have a look at a couple of examples:

char ch = names[0]; // Get value.

names[1] = 'A';    // Set value.

If a negative index is specified, or one that is >= (greater than or equal to) the value that the length property returns, Java will create an exception object and throw it. That exception object is:

**java.lang.ArrayIndexOutOfBoundsException**

# Chapter 10: Strings in Java

A string is nothing more than a sequence of characters that is terminated by the null character, to denote that the string has indeed been terminated.

In Java a string is denoted by the string data type.

Let's revisit how to define a string in Java via an example.

With the above program:

We are first defining a variable 'str' to be of the 'string' type.

Then we assign a string of "Hello World" to the 'str' variable.

Finally we output the value to the console accordingly.

With this program, the output is as follows:

The value of the string is Hello World

There are a variety of functions available in Java to work with strings. Let's look at them in more detail.

## 4.1 Length Function

This function is used to return the length of the string. Let's look at an example of this function.

With the above program:

We are using the 'length' method to get the length of the string.

With this program, the output is as follows:

The length of the string is 11

## 4.2 toLowerCase Function

This function returns the string in lower case. Let's now look at a simple example of this.

With this program, the output is as follows:

The lower case of the string is hello world

## 4.3 toUpperCase Function

This function returns the string in upper case. Let's quickly look at an example of this.

With this program, the output is as follows:

The lower case of the string is HELLO WORLD

## 4.4 Contains Function

This function is used to check the existence of another string, and returns True or False. Below is an example of this function.

With this program, the output is as follows:

Does the string contain Hello - True

## 4.5 endsWith Function

This function can be used to check whether a string ends with a particular string value. Let's now look at a simple example of this function.

With this program, the output is as follows:

Does the string end with World - true

# 4.6 indexOf Function

This function is used to get the index of a character in a string. Let's have a look at an example of this.

With this program, the output is as follows:

The index value of e is 1

# 4.7 Replace Function

This function is used to replace a character in the original string. Below we'll look at an example of this function.

With this program, the output is as follows:

The value of the string is Hello Again

# 4.8 Substring Function

This function is used to return a substring from the original string. Let's look at a quick example of this function.

With this program, the output is as follows:

The value of the string is Hello

If the value is less than zero it means that the destination string precedes the value.

If the value is greater than zero it means that the destination string follows the value.

If the value is equal to zero then this instance has the same position in the sort order as the value.

Let's now look at an example of this function.

With this program, the output is as follows:

The output of the compareTo function is 0

# Chapter 11: Java Web Development

## What are Java Web Applications?

Java web applications are, quite simply, web apps built using Java. But, much more than that, they are applications that generate web pages that are fully interactive, each containing different markup language types, such XML, HTML, and so on, along with dynamic content.

Typically, a Java web application will be made up of web components that modify data temporarily store the data, interact with web services and with databases and will render content as requested by the application users.

Some of the components are JSP – JavaServer Pages, JavaBeans and servlets.

Many of the tasks that are required for the development of web applications can be somewhat repetitive or they may require huge amounts of boilerplate code.

We can use web frameworks to take away some of the overhead that goes with the common development activities, for example, many of the frameworks include useful libraries that help you with page templating, session management and they often promote the reuse of code.

# What is Java EE?

Java Enterprise Edition (Java EE) is one of the most commonly used platforms and it contains a range of coordinated technologies that take some of the complexity and cost out of the development of server-centric, multi-tier applications, making it much easier to deploy them and manage them.

Java EE builds on Java SE and gives us a full set of development APIs that help us run server-side applications that are fully secure, portable scalable, robust, and reliable.

Some of the basic components include:

● EJB (Enterprise JavaBeans) – fully managed server-side architecture for enclosing application business logic. With EJB technology, we can rapidly develop Java-based applications that are distributed, secure, transactional and portable in a simplified way

● JPA (Java Persistence API) – a framework that provides ORM (Object-Relational Mapping) for data management capabilities within applications built using Java technology.

# Ajax Development with JavaScript

JavaScript is used mainly in the client-side user interfaces in web applications and is an object-oriented language.

Ajax, with stands for Asynchronous JavaScript and XML, is a technique that provides the ability for web pages to change without having to refresh the page each time.

JavaScript toolkits can easily be used to implement components enabled by Ajax, along with their functionality, right into a web page.

# The Practicalities of Developing Web Applications

Now it's time to get practical because that's the only real way to learn how to build a web application in Java. We're going to look at the basics of using the NetBeans IDE, how to produce a very simple web application, how to deploy it and how to see it in a web browser.

This application will use a JSP page for name input and a JavaBeans component to ensure the name persists throughout the HTTP session, retrieving that name so it can be output on the next JSP page.

The first place to start is in setting up your environment so you can follow along.

The software and resources you will need are:

- The NetBeans IDE – v 7.2 onwards, Java EE
- Java Development Kit – v 7 onwards
- Glassfish Server Open Source Edition v 4 onwards OR
- Tomcat Servlet container v 7 onwards OR
- Oracle Web Logic Server – v 10 onwards


If you opt for the Java EE version, you can easily install both the Glassfish and Apache Tomcat servlet containers.

Set Up Your Project

Once you have downloaded everything from above, you can follow this tutorial. Start by opening the NetBeans IDE

Click on File>New Project in the main menu or click CTRL+SHIFT+N if you prefer to use keyboard shortcuts.

Now click on Categories and choose Java Web

Click Projects>Web Application>Next

Go to the text box for Project Name and call it HelloWeb.

Decide the Project Location – it can be any directory on your system. For this tutorial we will be referring to the directory as $PROJECTHOME.

This is an optional step – check the box beside Use the Dedicated Folder for Storing Libraries and decide where the libraries folder will go.

Click on Next and a panel for the Server and Settings will open. Choose which Java EE version you are going to use with the application

Next, choose which server you are going to use for deployment of your application.

Note that you will only see those servers that are registered with the NetBeans IDE. Also note the Context Path (on server) changes to /HelloWeb/ - this is indicative of the name you provided earlier.

Click on Finish

NetBeans IDE will now create a project folder called $PROJECTHOME/HelloWeb.

If you go to the Files window in NetBeans or press CTRL+2, you can see the file structure for this project; go to the Projects window, or press CTRL+1 and you can see the logical structure.

This project folder is where all of your metadata and source will go for this project. HelloWeb will open directly in NetBeans IDE while the Welcome page, which is index.jsp, will open in the main window in the Source Editor.

Note – The NetBeans IDE may generate the default welcome page as index.html but this will depend on which server and which version of the Java EE that you chose when the project was created. You have two choices – follow this tutorial using the index.html file or go to the New File wizard and create an index.jsp file – if you choose the latter, make sure you delete index.html to avoid confusion.

Create and Edit Application Source Files

The NetBeans IDE serves many useful functions but one of the most important is the creation and editing of the source files for your web application.

That, in all honesty, is what most web app developers spend the bulk of their time doing.

With the IDE, you get a huge selection of tools that will suit all types of developer and the individual style that they have, regardless of whether you prefer the IDE to generate much of the code or whether you prefer to code manually.

# Chapter 12: Making our Program Interactive

## How to displaying output

The floating type represents fractional numbers. The floating types exist in two types, the double and float. The double represents the double precision numbers while the float represents the single precision numbers.

The double is applied frequently since functions of mathematics use double value. For instance, sqrt() will output a double. You can check its application in the code below. In this example, sqrt() has been applied to calculate the longest side of a triangle when the length of the other sides has been provided.

```
/*
   Use the Pythagorean theorem to
   find the length of the hypotenuse
   given the lengths of the two opposing
   sides.
*/
class Hypot {
  public static void main(String args[]) {
    double x, y, z;

    x = 3;
    y = 4;                    Notice how sqrt() is called. It is preceded by
                              the name of the class of which it is a member.
    z = Math.sqrt(x*x + y*y);

    System.out.println("Hypotenuse is " +z);
  }
}
```

The output from the program is shown here:

```
Hypotenuse is 5.0
```

We need to notice in the example above that **sqrt()** belongs to the **Math** class. But, notice the way the **sqrt()** has been used: first, it has been preceded by the **Math** name. Now, for **sqrt()**, it is similar.

# Converters

If you have programmed in another language, you might be thinking that characters in Java are 8. No! Java has Unicode. What a Unicode does is to define a set of characters which represents characters existing in the human languages.

The example below demonstrates:

Char th;

th = 'Y';

Still, if you want to display a char value by applying the **println()** statement. This example will show you how to do it:

System.out.println("This is th: "+ th);
Given that the char is unsigned 16-bit type, you can do some arithmetic operations in the char variable. For instance, look at the program below:

Class CharArith {
Public static void main (String args []) {
Char th;
th = 'X';
System.out.println("th has "+ th);
th++; // we increment the th, it is possible to increment a char
System.out.println("th is now "+ th);
th = 90; // we assign th the value Z
System.out.println("th is now "+ th);
}
}
Here is the output of the above program:
"th has X"
"th is now Y"
"th is now Z"

This program assigns variable **th** the value '**X**'. Then, it is incremented to **Y**, which is the next character in the Unicode sequence.

# Formatting outputs

In Java, the Boolean type refers to false or true values. Java finds out if it is true or false using the reserved keywords. Therefore, an expression

Boolean type will assume one of these values. An example to demonstrate include:

```
class BoolPro {
public static void main (String args []) {
  boolean q;
q = false;
System.out.println ("q is "+ q);
q= true;
System.out.println("q is "+ q);
// a boolean value can also control the if statement
If(q)
System.out.println("This is executed.");
q = false;
if(q)
System.out.println("This is not executed");
// Describe the results of the relational operator
System.out.println("11 > 8 is "+ (10 > 8));
}
}
The output:
 q is false
q is true
This is executed
11 > 8 is true
```

There are a few things to note about this program.

First, the **println()**, displays a boolean value. Secondly, the boolean values control the flow of an if statement.

You don't need to go the long way in writing the boolean type this way: **if (b == true)**

The result shown by the operator such as < is boolean. It is one of the reasons why we have the expression **11 > 8** showing the value **true**. In addition, the other pair of parentheses near the **11 > 8** is important since plus comes before the >.

# Escape sequences

Surrounding them with single quotes works for the majority of printing characters. However, there are certain characters which have a problem with the text editor.

Furthermore, double and single quotes tend to have a unique meaning to Java. T

his means you cannot just use them directly. Now, because of the above reason, Java has specific escape sequences, sometimes it is called a **backslash character constant**. This table illustrates:

| Escape Sequence | Description |
| --- | --- |
| \' | Single quote |
| \" | Double quote |
| \\ | Backslash |
| \r | Carriage return |
| \n | New line |
| \f | Form feed |
| \t | Horizontal tab |
| \b | Backspace |
| \ddd | Octal constant (where ddd is an octal constant) |
| \uxxxx | Hexadecimal constant (where xxxx is a hexadecimal constant) |

# Chapter 13: Control Flow Statements

When we talk about conditional logic, we are mostly talking about the IF word.

For example, IF user is younger than 18 then display this message; IF user is older than 18, display this message. Luckily, you will find that using conditional logic in Java is easy so let's begin by looking at IF statements.

## IF Statements

One of the most common things in computer programming is to execute code when one thing happens instead of something else.

Run the program and check it – Note that NetBeans tends to run the program in bold text in the window for Projects, not the code that you displayed.

If you want the code run in your coding window, right-click on the code, anywhere and then click on **Run File** in the menu that appears. The output will now appear in the Output window.

Next, we change the user variable value from 17 to 18; now run the program again.

You should see that the program runs fine, no errors but nothing will be printed.

The reason for this is because the message is in between the curly brackets in the IF statement and that statement is looking for values of lower than 18. If the condition isn't met, Java will ignore the curly brackets and anything in between them, moving on to the rest of the code.

We have previously looked at nested scopes; now we want to look at nested ifs. You will interact most of the time with a nested if. The greatest lesson to learn is nested ifs point to the block of code with the else.

Read the following example:

```
If( i ==10) {
If ( j < 20) a = b;
If (k > 100) c = d;
else a - c; // this else will point to the if (k > 100)
}
else a = d; //this else will point to the if (i ==10)
|
```

You should be able to note that the last else has not been associated with if(j<20), but associated with the if(i==10).

100

## IF ... ELSE

If you don't want to use two IF statements, there is another way -and IF ... ELSE statement.

So, we have two choices in this code – the user is either 18 or younger, or older than 18.

Change your code so it matches what is above and try it.

You should now see that the first message is printed out. Change the user variable value to 20 and then run the code again.

You should see the message that is between the curly brackets for ELSE displayed in the Output window.

## IF ... ELSE IF

The first IF statement will test for the first condition, then we have the ELSE IF, followed by parentheses, in between which goes condition two. If there is anything that the first two conditions do not catch, it will be caught by the last ELSE. Again, we have sectioned the code using curly brackets and each IF, Else IF or ELSE has its own set. If you miss out any of these curly brackets, you will get an error message.

Before you try out any more code, you must first learn about a few more conditional operators. So far, you have used these ones:

- **< - Greater Than**
- **< - Less Than**
- **>= - Greater Than or Equal To**
  - <u>**<= - Less Than or Equal To**</u>

Here's four more you can use:

- **&& - AND**
- **|| - OR**
- **== - HAS A VALUE OF**
- **! - NOT**

The first one, a pair of ampersand symbols, is used for testing two or more conditions at once.

We are checking to see if a user is older than the age of 18 but younger than the age of 40 – remember, we are checking what is in the variable called user.

The first condition, "greater than 18"; the second condition, "less than 40". Between those two conditions, we have the AND operator so the entire line is saying else if user is greater than 18 AND user is less than 40.

Now run the program and test it again; before it runs you should already be able to guess what is going to print.

The user variable has a value of 21 so the message that is between the else if curly brackets will show in the output window.

## Nested IF Statements

Look at where the curly brackets are – get one set in the wrong place or miss one out and the code will not run. Nested IF statements might be a little tricky but, really, all you are doing is narrowing the choices down.

# Boolean Values

Instead of using int, double or string, you would simply type in boolean (lower case b) and, after the variable name, you assign a TRUE or FALSE value.

Notice that we use a single equal sign as the assignment operator.

If you wanted to see if a variable "has a value of", you would need to use a pair of equals signs.

This time, we have used the NOT operator in front of the variable called user.

The NOT operator is indicated by the use of an exclamation mark, just one, and it will be placed in front of the variable that you are trying to test.

This operator tests for negation, which means that it is testing for the opposite of the actual value.

# Switch Statements

Another way of controlling flow is to use a switch statement. This provides you with the option of testing for a range of values for the variables and can be used in place of complicated, long IF … ELSE statements.

Start with the word "switch" and then a set of parentheses. The variable you are checking is placed between the switch parentheses and is followed by a set of curly brackets.

The rest of the switch statement goes in between the curly brackets.

# Chapter 14: Java GUI Programming

Assuming that the reader is not a total newbie to programming, and has been introduced to the world of programming using C or another procedural – heavy language, the next logical question would be: why even use object – oriented programming?

Well, one of its main advantages is that in the long run, it saves time.

## How to build a small game with Java

Procedural programming is usually much quicker and more straightforward in simpler algorithms and programs; rather than having to construct and define a class, and create an object based on that class, all the programmer really has to do is to simply declare the necessary variables and write the functions, and create the algorithm in order to solve the problem that they need the code to address.

However, when it comes to more complex programs, needing more complex solutions, this is where object – oriented programming begins to shine, and this is where it starts to show its strength. In a lot of programs, there will be times that there will be a number of "objects" or data clusters that have to be grouped together, and that the programmer will be treating in a certain way.

This is what "classes" are meant to address. Instead of declaring a new set of variables per data cluster, they can simply draw on a pre – made "class" and create a new "object". Let's see how this would work in practice.

Each piece also has different methods of moving, depending on what piece they are.

If a programmer were to code a chess game in procedural fashion, then they would have to manually describe each and every piece, all sixteen pawns, four bishops and four knights, four rooks, two queens, and two kings.

In addition, they will have to write the functions that allow each piece to move in its own separate way.

However, if the programmer makes use of object - oriented programming, instead of having to code sixteen pawns, four bishops, four knights, four rooks, two queens, two kings, they simply have to code six classes: one class to describe each piece on the board.

The programmer can now simply include the movement functions within each class, and have the attributes describe their position: whether they're white king's pawn, or black queen's pawn, these are all things that can be inserted through the "attributes" portion of the "pawn" class. Instead of thirty – two clusters of code, the programmer only has to do six.

Now it's much easier, much shorter, and also much more elegant.

# Chapter 15: Object Oriented Programming

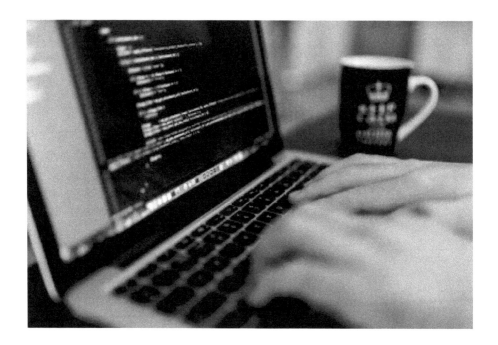

We're not going to tackle all the complex coding of object-oriented programming right now.

We're just going to be dealing with the raw concepts at heart: classes and objects. In order to understand these, we must first discuss classes.

This will make some of the things that we said earlier – like object wrappers – make more sense.

What is a class?

The utility of classes comes from the fact that sometimes you need more complex structures than what the code automatically gives you.

This occurs rarely in languages like JavaScript. Object-oriented programming is about this abstraction at its core: the ability to take smaller concepts and then integrate them into bigger structures that utilize these concepts.

A better way to think about it is to try to imagine a dog.

All dogs have features in common; for example, they have 2 eyes, 4 legs, and a wagging tail.

They can also bark. However, there can be a lot of variance, too.

For example, dogs can have separate breeds and other things which set them apart, like their size or weight.

However, there are still unifying concepts and properties that apply to all dogs, regardless their breed, size, and weight, which are **properties** they all have in common.

These can be portrayed as individual data members of a larger structure. This structure can be referred to as a **dog**.

These individual data members are called the properties of the dog class.

Each class can also have standard functions, like **bark** or **wagTail**, which are common among all instances of the class.

A singular instance of a class is referred to as an object.

Each object has its own name and can be treated as its own variable. So, if you define a class **dog**, you can create a dog variable known as **myDog** or any other standard variable name.

Then, access the properties and alter them however you wish.

This standardization and abstraction are the major appeals of object-oriented programming.

Therefore, whenever something is referred to as an **object**, it means that a class was constructed which consists of smaller data types and pieces of data that all make up the bigger concept that is represented both through the object and through its constituent class.

With that, we've worked through the bulk of the stuff that you need to know as an new JavaScript programmer.

These are the foundations of all the knowledge you gained from this book, and it's important that you understand all these before continuing.

# Java encapsulation

Information hiding is one of the key features of the Java programming language and object oriented programming. You have already been introduced to this concept in part we covered concepts on data abstraction. Simply put, an object in Java will usually hide how it implements its own functionality.

Now, in order to do that, you will have to make use of access control modifiers. Here are four of them:

- Public

- Private

- Protected

- Default

You are already familiar with the first two – public and private.

When the variable is declared to be public then it can be anywhere in the program you are writing. In contrast when it is private then it can't be seen or accessed anywhere else but in the body of the class where it has been instantiated.

Let's move on to the other two access control modifiers.

The next one on the list is called "protected" – which is useful in case you want to create libs. When a variable is protected, it means that it can only be seen within the package where this Java construct has been instantiated – note that this also includes all the subclasses.

The "default" access control modifier, on the other hand, is used by the variable when the other three aren't specified. In this mode, a variable can be accessed within package or class where it has been instantiated by the programmer. However, do take note that the variable is only accessible within the main body of the class and it is not available within its subclasses.

Note that you can also create an object within a method and the usual rules apply – the object or variable can only be accessed within the body of the method where it has been created.

Here's another important point that you should remember about variables that you create within a method – it can only specify one keyword for it: final.

You will not be allowed to create a default, protected, public, or even a private variable within the method body. And that is basically how information is hidden in your code, which, if you observe, facilitates data abstraction and encapsulation.

Encapsulation? Information Hiding? What's the Difference? It would appear at first glance that encapsulation and data or information hiding may look the same, but there is indeed a subtle difference between these two terms.

Now, Nat Pryce and Steve Freeman has made quite an accurate distinction between these two although you may read from other authors who use these terms interchangeably.

We'll use Freeman and Pryce's descriptions here to draw the difference between these two concepts in Java programming. Let's begin with information hiding since that is where we left off.

You can already judge what "information hiding" means. It simply means information is concealed. The actual functions and procedures performed by the program are concealed.

But, for what purpose? Why are the inner workings kept hidden from the programmer?

The lower level details are ignored so that you, the programmer, can focus on much more important things. That is also why data is abstracted in Java.

You can create classes, objects, and other elements of your program; you can even import objects from one program to another without worrying about the details on how that object does what it does.


It's like driving a car.

All you need to know is that when you insert your key into the keyhole and start the car, it will start.

You don't have to worry about what makes it start, how the wires are connected underneath there, where the gas goes, how the engine burns the gas, etc.

All you need to worry about is starting the car and driving safely.

Encapsulation, on the other hand, allows the user to control the amount of change in an object can affect the other parts of class.

The term "encapsulate" means to enclose everything in a singular cell.

That means that given the way the Java programming system is designed, there will be no expected dependency from one independent cell to another.

Remember that objects within the Java programming environment are meant to be stand alone, and there are no global variables to reference.

# Abstraction

**Abstraction** simply refers to the process of hiding unnecessary details of an object and only showing the ones that are relevant. **Encapsulation** on the other hand simply means the binding of the states and the methods of an object together.

This binding eventually creates something called a class (we'll cover that in a little bit). Finally, **message passing** refers to the ability of objects to interact with other objects.

High – level programming languages, on the other hand, have a much higher level of abstraction, meaning that code goes through a program called a compiler, which acts as the computer's translator, before the computer is able to use it.

This level of abstraction is usually to the point where the programming language already has syntax similar to English, a global language.

The compiler assumes the role of the translator between the high – level language and the machine.

This allows the programmer to write their program in a more natural manner, as it allows for the coder to use more "natural" language, and the higher – level language allows for some functions to be automated, making life much easier for the coder.

The trade – off here however is that the code has to go through a compiler, which will take lengthier for the program to run and execute, and the computer will often use more memory as compared to a lower – level language. Amongst these high – level languages are the more frequently – known ones, such as Python, C++, and our topic for today, Java.

# Chapter 16: Java Interview Questions

## The Java Programming Language

What is the WORA principle? Why is it beneficial?

How can Java applications run on multiple platforms?

What is the difference between the JRE and the JDK?

What is the difference between procedural programming and object-oriented programming?

## Object-Oriented Programming (Part I)

What is the difference between a class and an object?

What happens when an object is instantiated for the first time?

What is the difference between a primitive type and an object?

What is the difference between autoboxing and unboxing?

What is an array?

How is a String different from a regular object?

What is the difference between a StringBuilder and a StringBuffer?

Why are enums superior to String or Integer constants?

What is the difference between package-by-layer and package-by-feature?

# Object-Oriented Programming (Part II)

What is the difference between a method declaration and a method signature?

What is a recursive method?

What is the final keyword used for?

What is the static keyword used for?

Why can't a static method access a nonstatic field?

What are access modifiers used for? What are the different types?

What are annotations used for?

# The Object Superclass

What is the difference between a shallow copy and a deep copy?

Why is a copy constructor preferable to the clone method?

What is the difference between the identity operator and the equals() method?

What is the relationship between the hashCode() method and the equals() method?

What is the default implementation of the toString() method?

Why is the finalize() method unreliable for cleanup operations?

# Composition & Inheritance

What is the difference between composition and inheritance?

What is the difference between method overriding and method overloading?

How would you determine whether to use composition or inheritance?

# Abstract Classes & Interfaces

What is the difference between an abstract class and an interface?

How would you determine whether to use an abstract class or an interface?

Why can't a class be declared both final and abstract?

What is the value of designing a codebase around the use of interfaces?

What are anonymous classes used for?

What is a closure?

What is a lambda expression?

## Exceptions

What is an exception?

What is the difference between an unchecked and a checked exception?

How would you determine whether to use an unchecked or a checked exception?

How does a try/catch/finally block work?

How does the try-with-resources statement work?

# Generics

What is the difference between a compile-time error and a runtime error?

What is the purpose of generics?

What are the different types of generic wildcards?

What is type erasure?

What are some of the limitations of generics?

# Concurrency

What is the lifecycle of a Thread?

Why is synchronization necessary on shared resources?

What is used as a lock for synchronized static and synchronized non-static methods?

What would happen if two different threads hit two synchronized non-static methods on the same object simultaneously?

What would happen if two different threads hit a synchronized static method and synchronized non-static method on the same object simultaneously?

What one thing does the volatile keyword guarantee about a variable?

What two things does the synchronize keyword guarantee about a block of code?

What are some built-in concurrent data structures?

What is the executor framework?

What is a ThreadLocal variable?

What are atomic variables?

# Memory Management

How does the JVM divide memory on the heap?

What is the standard algorithm for garbage collection?

What are memory leaks? How can they be identified?

What are the four different types of references?

What is a ReferenceQueue?

Why is a phantom reference safer than using the finalize() method?

# Java Database Connectivity

What is JDBC?

What are the two ways of acquiring a Connection object?

What is the difference between the three types of Statements?

What is a ResultSet?

What is an SQL injection attack? How can it be prevented?

What are the advantages and disadvantages of object-relational mapping?

What is Hibernate?

# Web Applications

What is a servlet container?

What is a web application?

What is a WAR file?

What is a web.xml file?

What is the difference between a Servlet and an HttpServlet?

What is the difference between a Servlet and a JSP?

What is a servlet filter?

What is the model-view-controller pattern?

# Web Services

What is service-oriented architecture?

What are web services?

What is the difference between a SOAP web service and a REST web service?

What is the difference between JAX-WS and JAX-RS?

What are some frameworks that aid in the development of Java web services?

# Algorithms

What is Big O notation? What are some common examples?

What is a binary search? How well does it perform?

What is insertion sort? How well does it perform?

What is merge sort? How well does it perform?

What is quicksort? How well does it perform?

What is timsort? How well does it perform?

## Java Collections Framework

What is the difference between an ArrayList and a LinkedList?

How does a HashMap work internally?

What would happen if a key's hashCode() or equals() method was incorrect?

What is the difference between a stack and a queue?

What is the difference between a binary search tree, red-black tree, and a heap?

What is the difference between a HashSet, LinkedHashSet, and TreeSet?

What is the difference between a fail-fast iterator and a fail-safe iterator?

# Streams

What is the Stream API and why is it useful?

What is the difference between intermediate operations and terminal operations?

Why is the order of intermediate operations important?

What is the difference between parallel streams and sequential streams?

# Java Time_

What is the Java Time-Scale?

What is the difference between a LocalDateTime and a ZonedDateTime?

What is the difference between an Instant, OffsetDateTime, and ZonedDateTime?

What is the difference between a Period and a Duration?

# Important Interfaces

What is the Autocloseable interface?

What is the Comparable interface?

What is the Comparator interface?

What is the Iterable interface?

What is the Runnable interface?

What is the Callable interface?

What is the Serializable interface?

What is a functional interface? What are some common functional interfaces?

# Creational Design Patterns

What is the builder pattern? When is it useful?

What is the factory pattern? When is it useful?

What is the abstract factory pattern? When is it useful?

What is the prototype pattern? When is it useful?

What is the singleton pattern? When is it useful?

## Structural Design Patterns

What is the adapter pattern? When is it useful?

What is the composite pattern? When is it useful?

What is the decorator pattern? When is it useful?

What is the facade pattern? When is it useful?

What is the flyweight pattern? When is it useful?

## Behavioral Design Patterns

What is the command pattern? When is it useful?

What is the observer pattern? When is it useful?

What is the strategy pattern? When is it useful?

What is the visitor pattern? When is it useful?

What is the null object pattern? When is it useful?

## Reflection

What is reflection?

What is type introspection?

What is a Class object?

What is a Field object?

What is a Method object?

What are some of the pros and cons of reflection?

# Dependency Injection

What is the inversion of control pattern?

What is the difference between a service locator and dependency injection?

What is the difference between constructor injection and setter injection?

What is the Spring container?

What are the different ways of configuring a Spring container?

What is the lifecycle of a Spring container?

# Aspect-Oriented Programming

What is the difference between a core concern and a cross-cutting concern?

What is aspect-oriented programming?

What is the difference between an interface proxy and an inheritance proxy?

What is the difference between runtime weaving and binary weaving?

What is the AspectJ library?

# Unit Testing

What is test-driven development? Why is it beneficial?

What is a unit test?

What is JUnit?

What are text fixtures?

What are mock objects?

# Programming Problems

How would you write a method that calculates the factorial of a number?

How would you determine whether a string is a palindrome?

Given a line of text, how would you verify that the number of open and closed parentheses are balanced?

Given an unsorted list with one missing number from 1 to 100, how would you determine the missing number?

# Personal Questions

Could you tell us about yourself and your experience?

Could you tell us about any side projects you've worked on?

Could you tell us about a time you solved a particularly challenging problem?

Could you tell us about a time you resolved a disagreement with a coworker?

What was your previous development environment like?

Why you are interested in working at our company?

Why you are leaving your previous job?

What is your biggest weakness? What is your biggest strength?

# Chapter 17: Java Language and Terminology

## Absolute filename

An absolute filename is a filename with a full path that is provided from the top or the root of the file system tree, or example c:\Java\bin\javac.exe

## Abstraction

Abstraction is a simple representation of a complex situation. In basic terms, abstraction hides how a section of code or program works and shows only the functionality of it. This is designed to make it easier to maintain, read and work on the code. OOP design often revolves around finding an abstraction level to work with when real-life objects are being modeled. Too high a level and insufficient detail is capture; too low and you run the risk of a program being more complicated to create and difficult to understand that it should be.

## Abstract method

An abstract method is a method whose header contains the reserved keyword, abstract. Abstract methods do not have a method body. Any method that has been designed inside an interface is considered abstract, with no exceptions. An abstract method's body is defined inside an abstract class subclass or, if a class implements the interface, within that class.

## Abstract Windowing Toolkit

The AWT, or Abstract Windowing Toolkit contains a collection of classes that are designed to make creating applications with GUIs (graphical user interface) much simpler. You will find these in the java.awt group of packages and classes included are for buttons, windows, menus, frames, text areas and more.

## Accessor method

An accessor method is a method that has been designed specifically to provide access to a class private attribute. By Java convention, accessor methods are prefixed with get and then the attribute name. For example, to gain access to an attribute called speed, the accessor method would be getSpeed(). When attributes are set as private, it stops objects from external classes from modifying the value unless a mutator method is used. We can use accessor methods to provide specific access to the private attribute values and to stop other objects in other classes from accessing the private attribute – the correct visibility needs to be used for the accessor to achieve this.

## Actor

See client.

Actual argument

This is the value of the argument passed from outside a method into a method. When the method is called, the values (actual argument) will be copied to the formal arguments that correspond to it. The actual argument type and the formal argument types must be compatible with one another.

## Actual parameter

See actual argument.

Address space

This is the virtual memory area that a process runs in.

## Agent

See server.

## Aggregation

This is an OOP concept, a type of relationship where one object has at least one other subordinate object making up its state. These subordinate objects don't tend to have an independent existence outside the object that contains them. When this object no longer has a reason to exist, neither do its subordinates. For example, you may have a GasStation object that has a few pump objects. Once the GasStation object is destroyed or has no further use, the pump objects follow suit. Aggregation is also known as a HAS-A relationship, distinguishing form inheritance which is an IS-A relationship.

## Aliases

Aliases are several references to one object. The object may receive messages from any of the aliases and any change in state the results from a message will be easily detected by all.

## Anonymous array

This is an array that has been created with no identifier. Anonymous arrays tend to be created as actual arguments like this:

// An anonymous array of integers is created

YearlyRainfall y2k = new YearlyRainfall(

new int[]{ 10, 8, 9, 9, 5, 3, 2, 0, 3, 3, 8, 11}

);

Anonymous arrays can also be returned as the result of a method.

## *Anonymous class*

An anonymous class is one that does not have a class name. this type of class is generally a subclass or an interface implementation and normally gets created as an actual argument or is returned as a result of a method. For example:

quitButton.addActionListener(new ActionListener(){

public void actionPerformed(ActionEvent e){

**System.exit(0);**

  }

**});**

Anonymous object

An anonymous object is an object that gets created with no identifier. Usually, they are array elements, results of methods or actual arguments. For example:

private Point[] vertices = {

new Point(0,0),

new Point(0,1),

new Point(1,1),

new Point(1,0),

**};**

Also see anonymous class as, very often, anonymous objects come from anonymous classes

## *API*

See application programming interface.

Append mode

Append mode is a mode of file writing in which the contents of a file are kept when the file gets opened and new content gets appended.

## *Applet*

An applet is a small Java program that is based on the Applet or the JApplet class. Mostly they are used for providing active content on a web page and they have a number of features that set them apart from a standard Java graphical app, including security restrictions that limit them in what they can do and having no main method defined by a user.

## *Application*

Application is sometimes used synonymously for the word program but, as far as Java is concerned, application is the term used to describe GUI programs that aren't applets.

Application programming interface (API)

The API is a set of definitions used for writing a program. In Java, an API is a set of classes, packages and interfaces used for creating complex applications without having to start from the bottom up.

## *Argument*

An argument is the information or data passed to a method. Sometimes arguments are called parameters. If a method expects to be passed arguments the method header must have a declaration for a formal argument for every argument. When the method is called the values for the actual arguments are copied to the formal arguments that correspond with each one.

## *Arithmetic expression*

An arithmetic expression is one that contains numerical values that are of float or int type. For example, the arithmetic operators, like *, +, -, and /, will all take an arithmetic expression as an operand and their results are arithmetic values.

## *Arithmetic operator*

These are a type of operator that will return a numerical result and are part of an arithmetic expression. Operators include +, -, *, /.

## *Arpanet*

Arpanet is the network that came before the global internet.

## *Array*

An array is an object of fixed size that can hold at least zero items of the declared type for the array. For example, an int array will hold int items.

## *Array initializer*

An array initializer is used to initialize an array. It steps in to take the role of the separation creation step and the initialization. For example:

int[] pair = { 4, 2, };

is equivalent to the following four statements.

int[] pair;

pair = new int[2];

pair[0] = 4;

pair[1] = 2;

## Assembler

An assembler is a program that is used for translating programs that are written in the assembly language into a binary form of a specified instruction set.

## Assembly language

The assembly language is a symbolic one that corresponds very closely to a central processing unit (CPU) instruction set. The assembler (above) is the translation program that transforms the program into binary.

## Assignment operator

The assignment operator is an equal sign (=) used for storing an expression's value into a variable; for example, variable = expression. The right side of the operator must be evaluated before the assignment can be made. An assignment may, on its own be used on an expression. This example assignment statement will store a value of zero into both of the variables – x = y = 0.

## Assignment statement

An assignment statement is a statement that contains the assignment operator.

## Attribute

An attribute is a specific use of an instance variable. The attribute values in one class instance are defining the current state of that specific instance. Class definitions can impose constraints on the valid instance states through a requirement that a given attribute or attributes do not take particular values. For example, if an attribute holds exam results for a class, it should not have negative values. An attribute may be manipulated using mutator and accessor methods.

## Base case

A base case is a non-recursive route taken through a recursive method

Base type

The base type indicates the item type in an array, i.e. the arrays' defined type. For example:

int[] numbers;

Numbers have a base type of int. If the base case is the type of class, it will be indicating lowest supertype of the objects that the array can store. For example:

Ship[] berths;

All that can be stored in berths are instances of the class called Ship. If an array's base type is Object, it may be used for storing instances for any class.

## Behavior

Class methods are what implement the behavior of a class. The behavior of a specific object is a mixture of the class method definitions and the current state of the specific object.

## Big-endian

A type of machine. One of the most common differences between machines is how they store each byte of numerical data with many bytes. A big-endian machine will store high-order bytes first, followed by low-order bytes.

Also see little-endian

## binary

A binary is base 2 number representation. With base 2 only 1 and 1 are used as digits and the positions of the digits are representing successive powers of 2.

Also see bit

## Binary operator

A binary operator is an operator that will take two operands. Java has several binary operators, including some of the arithmetic and Boolean operators.

## Binary search

A binary search is a search that looks through sorted data where the central position is looked at first. The search will then go to the left or the right, eliminating the other side of the data space. This is repeated for each step until all the data has been searched or the specific item has been located.

## Bit

A bit is a binary digit. It can take only two values, 0 and 1. A bit is a basic block for building both data and programs. A computer will move data around on a regular basis in multiples of units made up of 8 bits, generally called bytes

Bit manipulation operator

A bit manipulation operator, like |, &, and ∧, are used for manipulating bits inside data item bytes. The <<, >> and >>> shift operators are bit manipulation operators too.

Blank final variable

A blank final variable is a final variable that wasn't initialized when it was declared. These variables need to be initialized in one of two ways before it can be used – in every class constructor or in an instance initialization block.

## *Block*

A block is a section of code made up of declarations and statements enclosed in a pair of opening and closing curly brackets {}. Both a class body and a method body are blocks. Blocks are also used for enclosing nested scope levels.

## *Bookmark*

A bookmark is used by a web browser as a way of remembering URL details.

## *Boolean*

a Boolean is a primitive data type in Java. It has just two possible values – TRUE or FALSE.

Boolean expression

a boolean expression is one that results in a boolean, i.e. TRUE or FALSE. The && and the | operators, among others, will take a boolean operand, producing a boolean result. Relational operators will take operands of different types and will also produce a boolean result.

## Boot

A computer "boots" up when you turn it on and the term is derived from the phrase "pulling yourself up by your bootstraps". When a computer is first switched on it must load everything it needs from its disks before it can be used but, to do this, there is a program it needs and this is called a bootstrap.

Bootstrap classes

A bootstrap class is part of the Java Platform Core API, like those from the java.io and java.lang packages.

Boundary error

A boundary error is one that happens as a result of a mistake happening at the edge of a problem, such as no items of data, indexing off an array edge, a loop termination and more. Boundary errors are very common logical errors.

Bounded repetition

Bounded repetition is where statements in the body of a loop get performed a certain number of times – the number of times is worked out when the loop begins. Java does not have any control structure that will guarantee bounded repetition.

Also see unbounded repetition

## Bounds

A bound is the limit of a collection or array. In Java, a lower limit will always be zero and, where arrays are concerned, an upper bound will always be one less than the array length and it is fixed. When you index outside a collection or array bound, you will get an IndexOutOfBoundsException thrown.

Branch instruction

A branch instruction will store an instruction address in the counter for a program. The result is that the next instruction fetched may not be the one that immediately follows the branch instruction and this causes disruption in the normal sequence of instruction execution. The result of this is conditional instruction execution and repetition.

## *Break statement*

A break statement is a statement for breaking out of a loop, a labeled block or a switch statement. In every case, control flow moves to the statement that immediately follows the block containing the statement.

Bridging method

A bridging method is one that provides a bridge between methods in a public interface for a class and the private implementation of that interface. Usually, bridging methods are non-public in terms of visibility.

## *Byte*

A byte is, in computing terms, eight data bits. In Java, it is also a primitive data type with a size of eight bits.

## *Bytecode*

The Java compiler translates Java source files into bytecode which is the instruction set of the JVM. All bytecode is stored in a .class file.

# CONCLUSION

I would like to thank you for choosing my guide on Java programming.

As you can see, it is a simple yet complex language, with so many different aspects to learn. By now you should have a good understanding of the core concepts of Java programming and how to use it.

Your next step is, quite simply, practice.

And keep on practicing. You cannot possibly read this guide once and think that you know it all.

I urge you to take your time going through this; follow the tutorials carefully and don't move on from any section until you fully understand it and what it all means.

To help you out, there are several useful Java forums to be found online, full of people ready and willing to help you out and point you in the right direction.There are also loads of online courses, some free and some that you need to pay for, but all of them are useful and can help you take your learning to the next level.

Did you enjoy this guide? I hope that it was all you wanted and more and it has put you on the right path to getting your dream job!

www.ingramcontent.com/pod-product-compliance
Lightning Source LLC
LaVergne TN
LVHW051243050326
832903LV00028B/2554